Tail TALK

Tail

TALK

UNDERSTANDING THE SECRET LANGUAGE OF DOGS

SOPHIE COLLINS

FOREWORD BY

DR KAREN L. OVERALL

BONNIER BOOKS

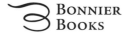

BONNIER BOOKS

First published in the United Kingdom in 2007 by Bonnier Books,
Appledram Barns, Birdham Road, Chichester PO20 7EQ

British Library Cataloguing-in-Publication Data
A catalogue record for this book is available from the British Library

ISBN-13: 978-1-905825-45-5

Website: www.bonnierbooks.co.uk

This book was conceived, designed and
produced by iBall, an imprint of Ivy Press

The Old Candlemakers
West Street, Lewes
East Sussex, BN7 2NZ, UK
www.ivy-group.co.uk

Creative Director Peter Bridgewater
Publisher Jason Hook
Editorial Director Caroline Earle
Senior Project Editor Hazel Songhurst
Art Director Sarah Howerd
Designers Clare Barber and Kevin Knight
Photographers Calvey Taylor-Haw and Simon Punter

Manufactured in China

CONTENTS

FOREWORD

How fluent is the average person in "dog"? In my experience, few people are sufficiently fluent in canine language to have the close, bonding relationship with their pet that they wish for. Sophie Collins has crafted a literate, readable and clear guide that attempts to open the world of canine communication from the dog's viewpoint – a glossary of "dog" that will help humans understand the basics of what their canine friends have been trying to tell them.

The fact that this book does not impose any preconceived – but usually scientifically ill-founded – belief structures about how dogs were, should be or would be, is of enduring value. It is clear from the photographs that once you know where to look, dogs are non-stop chatterboxes, always signalling, correcting, checking, reinforcing, clarifying, asking for information and acting upon that information.

All language acquisition is based on pattern recognition, whatever the species. The choice of dog vocabulary used in this book allows humans to watch and participate in the choreography that is canine signalling. Minute by minute, postures shift from one to another, making the dog's behaviour clear, understandable and elegant. Once you know what to look for, you will able to tell when a dog's response to meeting another dog differs substantially from the dog's "normal" greeting repertoire, and recognise how a normal pattern of exuberant behaviour in one dog can be misinterpreted as a threat by another dog.

So how do dogs communicate so well without a verbal language? There are two answers. The first is that they do it well because most confirmation that vocal signals have been understood is based in non-verbal signals (even for that most remorselessly noisy species – humans). The second is based on recent scientific findings that would have been laughed at a decade ago: dogs appear to use a form of "verbal" speech. In addition to indicating their relationship to other dogs and to humans using body postures and motion, dogs also vocalise with unique barks for different individuals. Didn't you ever wonder what made you know that when Scruffy barked that way, that Mum was home?

This book captures the wonderful complexity that is canine behaviour and invites the reader to share in it. Maybe if we let dogs teach us their language, we can finally reciprocate in the "best friend" relationship. If we are willing to really understand dogs from their viewpoints, I fully believe that people will have the best relationship possible with their pet, that dogs will be happier and that people will be changed for the better by what they have learned.

Karen L. Overall, MA, VMD, PhD
Diplomate ACVB
ABS Certified Applied Animal Behaviourist

INTRODUCTION

Numerous weighty tomes have been written about the language of dogs, many of which are like complete language courses: 30 hours of Berlitz, say, in Dog. *Tail Talk* is something simpler – a visual phrase book of Dog for those who have always wondered what their pets are saying. Naturally, it has its limitations: a modest 128 pages can't hope to contain years of research or much technical language. What it does do, however, is prompt you to look at your dog's language and begin to decipher what he or she may be saying to you. You might even gain some basic insights into what you are saying to him or her – it's not always what you think it is.

WORDS AND PHRASES

Humans use letters to make words, and words to make phrases, and speech is probably the most important means of communication for us. Dogs are different: "speech", in the sense of barks, whines, howls and other sounds is less crucial for them than many other aspects of their communication. Instead, they use tails, ears, eyes, whiskers, mouths and posture in order to tell us what they are thinking and, once you have some idea of what to look for, they are astonishingly eloquent. Sometimes they're hampered by their breed physique. For example, to the casual onlooker, it won't be obvious when a dog with very large pendant ears swivels them forwards or back. However, dogs have a number of communication tools at their disposal, and every dog is skilled in using all of them. There is no such thing as an inarticulate dog.

Tail Talk is divided in two parts. The first, "The Alphabet", looks at dogs from ears to tail and shows the range of different signs that can be sent by each part. In the second section, "The Phrase Book", we look at dogs and watch the ways in which they behave in different situations. Even in the artificial environment in which the pictures for this book were taken, it was astonishing to see the subtle and sophisticated range of signs used by the dogs, from the eight-month-old golden retriever to the nine-year-old collie. All of them used their language, dog to dog, with great individuality, not just in expressing likes and dislikes but in showing comfort, aggression, contentment, enthusiasm and even fear, often combining many signals to make a full picture.

SPECIES SPECIFICS

It's hard to look at dogs without anthropomorphism. In fact, it can be nearly impossible. Remember that trying to read what a dog is saying is not like trying to understand Italian – dogs aren't just another nationality, they're a whole different species. You're looking at something more fundamental than cultural differences. Even the language we use to describe dog talk is subjective because it has evolved to describe the feelings of people. Bear this in mind when you find yourself saying, "He's looking to me for protection", "She's showing how much she loves me" or "Look how jealous he's feeling!" You may be right, but, equally, you may be very wrong if you try to attribute human motivation to a species with overlapping but inherently different needs. You're inevitably speaking in Human, not Dog.

When we stop regarding dogs as quasi-human beings, we sometimes go to the other extreme and talk as though they are wild beasts, perpetually within a hair's breadth of tearing one another limb from limb. Dogs are pack animals – this is really just a word for a canine social grouping, but sometimes people assume that this means that in the wild they would be savagely fighting for their place in the pack. In reality, life in the wilderness is far too harsh for wild animals to be able to afford to fight much. The individuals in packs work cooperatively, and working relationships are usually defined by deferring to the individual best suited to a particular task in hand. When wild dog and wolf packs have been observed, the scientists doing the research noticed that the status quo is maintained by negotiation, expressed by numerous small signs sent in body language. Much of this body language is still recognisable in domestic dogs today; all you have to do is to learn what to look for, and often you'll see a whole social scene opening up to you as you take a walk in the park with your dog.

DIFFERENT SCENES, DIFFERENT CHARACTERS

Don't underestimate the individuality each and every dog brings to his or her communication. Just like people, dogs have their own characters, and much of their behaviour is just "how they are". When you say of a friend, "She loses her temper easily" or "He never stands up for himself", you'll be thinking of the language the friend uses (or sometimes doesn't use) to express those characteristics. Dogs are the same – there are several factors to their

communications. There are some generalities that you'll have heard about, which may be broadly true (terriers "are compulsive", bulldogs "don't back down"). These are often the result of characteristics that have been bred in to make certain types of dog better at a specific job, such as hunting or fighting. There is purely instinctive "language", too – signs that dogs don't give deliberately, but are just their natural reactions to a situation (raised hackles, face tension). And then, most interesting to the observer, there are the signs they use deliberately to tell others (dogs and sometimes people too) how they are feeling about a situation. This last is each dog's personal language, unique to that dog.

LEARN THE TALK

Tail Talk came about through a daily observation of many dogs interacting together. Any dog owner can learn to read their own dog better, and often to read other dogs, too. You can even learn to offer reinforcement or reassurance in ways that are familiar or recognisable to your dog. Dogs are intelligent, and yours may have learned a few human signals, but they'll always appreciate efforts to speak to them in their own language, and they make a forgiving audience. Your dog is talking to you – learn to listen.

THE ALPHABET

EARS

Most so-called "primitive" dog breeds have large, pointed ears
— not only do tall, open ears enable the dog to hear more clearly,
but they also make it easier for other dogs to see, even
at a distance, what their owner is expressing. Selective breeding
has made ears less universally easy to read, but even small or
long drop ears are still sending the same signals if you look
carefully. Dogs' ears swivel, moving backwards and forwards
and inwards or outwards, sometimes even falling
in different-shaped folds, according to emotion.
When dogs have hard-to-interpret ears, look at
the ear base — it shows clearly what position
the ear is really in.

A relatively small drop ear is concealed inside this Afghan's lavish fringing of hair.

This bloodhound is the possessor of seriously extravagant drop ears.

BELOW It's possible to "read" even the most extreme ear shapes — you can see from the base of the ear whether it's being held forward or back. This basset hound's ears are in neutral!

The medium-sized upright ears of this greyhound are easy to read, even at a distance.

Large, functional, expressive ears are characteristic of the German shepherd.

EARS ALERT

As a dog begins to develop interest in something his ears move forwards a little. In a dog with easy-to-read ears, this will be seen as a slight pricking up; in drop-ear dogs, you can see the position of the ear on the scalp change just a little. As the dog's interest intensifies, the ears move further forwards. The ear position is showing the degree of interest, but it doesn't tell you much about what the dog feels about what's provoking the reaction. The whole body posture will give you clues about whether the interest is anticipatory, slightly baffled or fearful. As the situation develops, the interest will either intensify — propelling the dog into action of some kind or another — or die back, whereupon the body language, and the ears, will return to neutral.

ABOVE Both dogs are in a mild-interest gear. Their ears are being held naturally, perhaps slightly forward. They are focusing on something directly in front of them. Open mouths with slightly lolling tongues reinforce the gentle interest the ears are showing.

MOVING TO INTEREST You can see the ears-alert position in the Lakeland terrier on the left. This little dog is a degree or two more excited than the Samoyeds on the facing page. His "button" ears (ears that fold forwards into a V-shape on the skull) are held well forward, indicating his interest, an interest that has started to get the rest of his body involved — tail held still but up, and head tilted slightly to one side. He's poised in the moment before action. It does not look as though the stimulus poses any threat — he still has that relaxed open mouth.

LEFT If you look very carefully, you can see that this Lakeland is not really sitting, but squatting, barely touching the ground, braced for action.

TAKING A BACK SEAT

When a dog is only mildly interested in something and has no plans for participation, the ears may be the main indicator of that interest. The German short-haired pointer, right, looked as though he'd rather be elsewhere. In this picture, his ears are tilted slightly forwards, but his mouth is closed (relaxed mouths tend to be open in dogs); the overall impression is one of mild uncertainty.

EARS BACK

When a dog pulls its ears completely back against its head, the signal is unambivalent — it is uncomfortable, and it is feeling apprehensive, aggressive or sometimes a mixture of both. An ear clamped to the head combined with a snarl is at the aggressive end of the scale; one pinned low to the head, combined with a closed mouth, is showing a more fearful response. None of the ears you see here are expressing anything as extreme as either of these signals. Ears turned slightly back can mean an increase in stimulus ("I just got more interested"), an increase in stress, as in the Jack Russell terrier below, or ambivalence ("I'm not sure where I am in this situation yet; I'm still making up my mind").

 LEFT This pointer is watching two other dogs getting rambunctious in play. His ears are moving back from their previous position, and his head tilt conveys a growing interest.

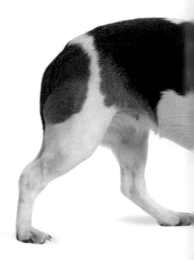

SENDING A WARNING If a dog feels that its space is being invaded, particularly by another dog, it will sometimes fold back its ears as part of a sequence of defensive, warning-off body signals. The sign may be accompanied by a lowered head and a hard look — to human eyes, the effect is slightly threatening but also uncertain. If the warned dog continues to be insensitive, the ears may go further back as the prelude to the issue of a much more forceful warning, usually a snarl or snap. Generally, it is the more naturally submissive dogs who issue the ears-back warning, and their body language may simultaneously be expressing anxiety; the sequence is not a confident one.

BELOW This fox terrier is eager and gregarious — sometimes too pushy — with other dogs. Here, he has just seen two new dogs entering the room: his ears have folded back in strong interest and he is assessing the possibilities. As soon as he is let loose, he will rush over and initiate a forceful introduction, whether it is welcomed or not.

This Jack Russell terrier is definitely uncomfortable. Her ears are back, and the tail tucked under.

● EARS IN CONTEXT

Both dogs on these pages are holding their ears back, but apart from this, their body language could not be more different. The fox terrier is heading towards a pair of dogs he hasn't met before; he's keen to introduce himself and initiate some play. His ears are expressing anticipation, curiosity and uncertainty, all at the same time. He's stepping out confidently, his tail is up, but he's holding it still (we'll come on to this later — it will start moving as soon as he has got some response), and his mouth is open, showing a relaxed tongue. There's no tension in his face: he is simply looking forward to meeting new dogs.

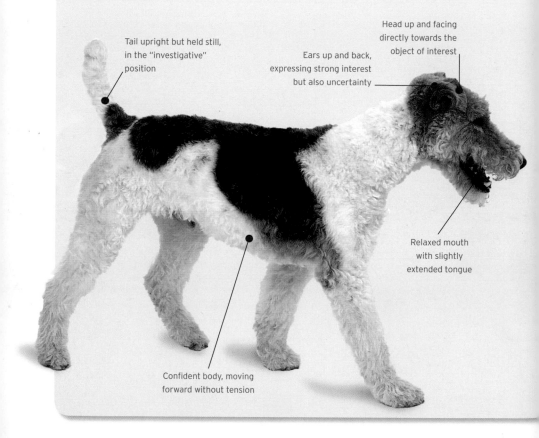

Tail upright but held still, in the "investigative" position

Ears up and back, expressing strong interest but also uncertainty

Head up and facing directly towards the object of interest

Relaxed mouth with slightly extended tongue

Confident body, moving forward without tension

In contrast, the Jack Russell terrier is feeling extremely apprehensive. Not naturally gregarious, she was being urged into a room where a group of dogs she hadn't met were already playing boisterously. Her body language is completely unambiguous: she doesn't want to go. She is pulling back with braced legs against her owner, who is encouraging her forward; her ears are fully back and down, and her whole body is expressing "I don't want to go." The topline of her body is also slightly rounded, which is characteristic of apprehension, fear or discomfort.

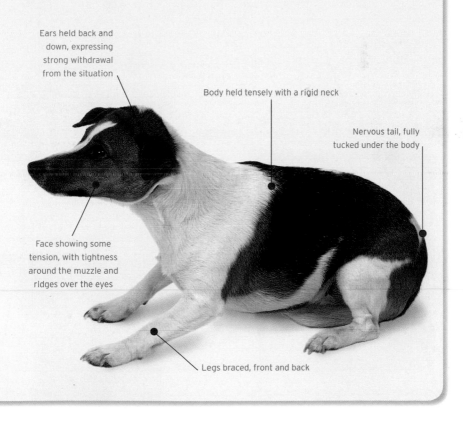

Ears held back and down, expressing strong withdrawal from the situation

Body held tensely with a rigid neck

Nervous tail, fully tucked under the body

Face showing some tension, with tightness around the muzzle and ridges over the eyes

Legs braced, front and back

EYES

We know less about how good dogs' vision is than we do about their scenting ability (their sense of smell is over forty times more acute than ours), although we know that dogs with "squashed" faces have a different retinal distribution from those with the long faces characteristic of sight hounds. Research has confirmed that a dog's field of vision changes according to the task for which it was bred: sight hounds — such as greyhounds, salukis and borzois — have better lateral vision than, say, the Boston terrier on the right. Although early dog breeds usually had relatively long and narrow-shaped eyes, many breeds today have been purposely developed with large, round eyes that lead people to think they have a more "human" expression — all the better to anthropomorphise!

ABOVE The Boston terrier is a popular companion breed in the United States. It was specially bred to have large eyes — owners like them because they give the dogs an empathetic, near-human expression.

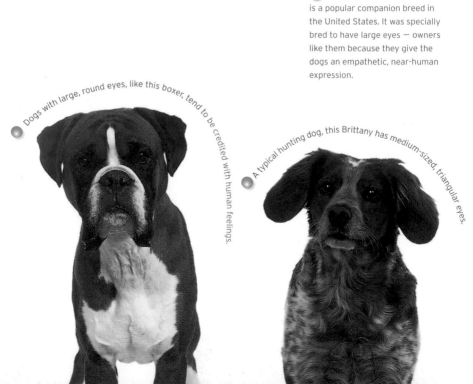

Dogs with large, round eyes, like this boxer, tend to be credited with human feelings.

A typical hunting dog, this Brittany has medium-sized, triangular eyes.

● LEFT The whippet, one of the so-called "sight hounds", is genetically predisposed to see prey in the distance, and to pursue it at high speeds.

The Old English sheepdog can see out, but its eye signals are likely to remain enigmatic.

Large, soft, oval eyes are characteristic of retrievers, like this English setter.

RELAXED EYES

Dogs who are contented or in neutral usually have rounded eyes, with a soft look. Like us, they also blink a lot — this distinguishes a relaxed look from a harder stare and sends other dogs a "no threat" message, helping meeting-and-greeting situations to stay relaxed. In play, or concentrating on something in particular, a dog's eyes sometimes crease up a little in a slight squint. This also acts as a friendly indication to other dogs. You see it when two dogs are play-wrestling with a toy; squinched-up eyes recognise that what is going on is fun, not conflict.

Although the Lakeland terrier is beginning to feel excited — with forward ears and tail held still — his eyes are rounded and relaxed.

This young retriever is totally relaxed, but she is squinting her eyes slightly in concentration as she noses out a treat.

FRIENDLY GLANCES

When a dog is around familiar faces in a comfortable situation, it will look closely and directly at what is going on. This can easily be distinguished from the "hard" stare of a dog who is giving a warning; It's a casual gaze and even when it's broadly focused on the same point it darts around. This pointer has finished playing and is relaxing (the open mouth, lolling tongue and neutral ears all tell us this). His rounded eyes complete the picture; there is no facial tension here.

BELOW This Jack Russell terrier is highly alert — head tilted, paw lifted, open slightly shortened muzzle. Her eyes are rounded and wide open. She's excited and anticipatory.

ALERT EYES

Something interesting has happened around the pointer on the opposite page, and it has adopted an alert pose. You see its behaviour change in an instant from reactive to proactive: it wants to investigate. Among the signs (which can also be read in the ears, tail and whole-body posture) is a broadening of the eyes, often a rapid blinking, and sometimes a tightening of the muscles in the face. In dogs with contrasting patches of colour above their eyes, you may also see the "eyebrows" rise and move in towards the nose — technically dogs don't have eyebrows, but the area of skin above their eyes can be read in much the same way as a human eyebrow. As with dogs' ears, the eyes offer an idea of the strength of reaction, but they don't automatically tell you whether that reaction is good or bad, happy or fearful. The overall expression, whole-body stance and the message the tail is sending will all need to be interpreted before you can be certain of what's coming next.

HARD-TO-READ FACES

Sometimes generations of breeding have created dogs with unusual faces that are harder to read than most. This bull terrier is playing hard with a good canine friend, chasing and barging, and is in cheerful, full-alert mode. However, you couldn't read this only from her eyes because their narrow shape isn't easily revealing. That's why it's important to read "whole-body" dog talk by putting different signals together.

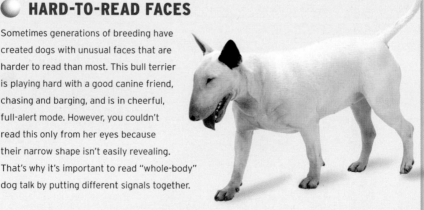

PUPIL POWER Like ours, the pupils of dogs' eyes react to exciting and frightening stimuli. In normal situations, you don't see much of the white of a dog's eye (it usually only shows as a narrow white rim when the dog is excited or stressed), but you can see a dog's pupils dilate as something engaging or provoking starts to happen. Although it's too quick to see when dogs are growing apprehensive or angry, there is a two-stage response (the pupils contract before dilating); but when they are happy or exhilarated, the pupils simply enlarge.

This pointer's pupils are dilated. With ears tipped forward, he looks at his owner holding a food treat.

Reprimanded by another dog, this terrier averts his eyes until things calm down.

AVERTED EYES

Humans are brought up to look each other in the eye — seen as a sign of trustworthiness — but not to hold prolonged eye contact, because staring is rude. To dogs, a "hard" direct look equals a stare, and it's a challenge. How they react varies, but this is one common cause of trouble between dogs and people who are not used to dogs; the latter meets and greets, looking straight at the dog, and the dog identifies the person as a threat. Polite dogs, when meeting, look at each other very briefly, then look past one another, averting their eyes. The message is one of negotiation, "I'm not a threat." After the preliminaries, the dogs may relate more closely, but the niceties have been observed. Contrast the in-your-face manner of the young Lakeland terrier, right, with the courteous, restrained demeanour of the Samoyed.

ABOVE The Lakeland terrier wants to play with the Samoyed and is pushing into her personal space. He knows he's taking a risk; his neck is slightly turned, deferentially, and you can see the whites of his eyes. Meanwhile, the Samoyed is averting her gaze and turning aside; she's not yet sure if she wants to play.

HEADS

Although the different shapes of various breeds' heads may seem wildly disparate at first sight, there are really only two fundamental shapes of head in dogs: that with a relatively narrow skull and a long snout, which is closer to the shape of the heads of the early feral dogs, and the wide, short, boxy head seen at its most extreme in the English bulldog and some breeds of mastiff. It's much easier to glean information from the facial expression and the position of the head of the longer-nosed dog; there are more obvious indications to work with. However, it is possible to read any dog's face if you learn some of the other body indicators and signs, too. There are some general rules that can be applied to most dogs to get you started.

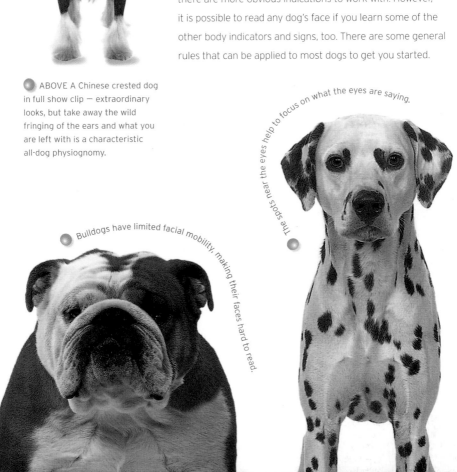

ABOVE A Chinese crested dog in full show clip — extraordinary looks, but take away the wild fringing of the ears and what you are left with is a characteristic all-dog physiognomy.

The spots near the eyes help to focus on what the eyes are saying.

Bulldogs have limited facial mobility, making their faces hard to read.

LEFT This English bull terrier displays the unusual egg-shaped head with very little facial skin mobility characteristic of the breed. You will need experience and practice to read his facial expression accurately.

With a long nose and visible "eyebrows", this Welsh terrier has an easy face to read.

A long muzzle and large open ears characterise this greyhound.

FACIAL TENSION

When dogs are in a reactive state or are in the process of becoming excited, the muscles of their faces tense up in various ways. This is one of the indicators that you need to learn to look for — it isn't immediately obvious to a casual glance. Depending on the degree of pressure a dog is feeling, you can see ridges of tensed muscle under the eyes, along the mouth and sometimes above the eyes, too. Remember that stress can be equivalent to excitement — although we tend to use it as a pejorative word, in this context it merely indicates that the dog is noticing and responding to one kind of stimulus or another.

 LEFT This terrier has just been startled by a noise. She's showing curiosity (muscle ridges above the eyes) and caution (legs bent, ready to move backwards).

◯ EYEBROWS?

Technically, dogs don't really have eyebrows. People have them to stop sweat dripping into their eyes, but dogs sweat from their soles, and cool down by panting, so they don't need them. However, the region above the eye has mobile muscles and sensory vibrissae (stiff, whisker-like hairs that are very sensitive). This pointer is showing slight tension, which is visible in small ridges and changes in the pile of his fur above his eyes.

 ABOVE You'll see a neutral face if you look carefully under and over the eyes and around the muzzle of this Labrador retriever. None of the musculature is showing through the fur. The expression of the eyes is soft and relaxed, too.

TIGHT MOUTHS Some aspects of dogs' mouth and tooth display are discussed on page 52, but dogs can also show stress around a closed mouth. If you've seen a dog growling — a low, single-pitch note that gets lower as it continues — or, even more serious, snarling, you'll have noticed that the face pleats into deep creases and the whiskers flare in tension. A growl is already a strong warning. Long before this point is reached, the dog will close his mouth (hiding the lolling tongue, which is usually a sign of comfort and relaxation) and tighten the musculature around his mouth, creating a shortened look to the nose. This is hard to see in pug-faced dogs, but is easily visible on a long face. Conversely, dogs that are particularly happy and relaxed tend to show "long" mouths, with extended, looser lips.

HEAD TILTS

The classic "what's going on?" pose, head tilts are a part of almost every dog's vocabulary. To us, the dogs may look quizzical, but the tilt acts as a marker between first noticing a stimulus and taking action — or, sometimes, deciding not to. Experts believe that the head tilt derived as a part of hunting behaviour; angling the head towards a noise may enable the dog to hear it more clearly — and some dogs have good ear mobility, too, so they can swivel their ears towards the sound. Head tilts are often seen in a pet that doesn't hunt, and seem to serve the same interested, curious function as a paw lift. In a working dog, the latter would be a hunting sign, but it can also be a simple sign of engagement or uncertainty.

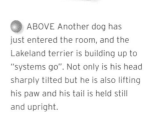

ABOVE Another dog has just entered the room, and the Lakeland terrier is building up to "systems go". Not only is his head sharply tilted but he is also lifting his paw and his tail is held still and upright.

RIGHT This collie shows curiosity with a relaxed mouth and tail, intent demeanour and slight head tilt.

LEFT This shy, elderly greyhound was acting as onlooker rather than participant. As other dogs appeared, she lowered her head and averted her gaze slightly, making it plain that she was only an observer, but her awareness of each new arrival was still evident in a small head tilt.

HEAD POSITIONS

Once you have learned the various messages that a familiar dog is sending through his ears, eyes and face, you can gain an overall picture from the position of the whole head. Popular lore says that the lower the head is held, the more "submissive" the message; but this is a simplification. A head held low and thrust forward can signal fearful aggression; but some dogs also hold their heads low to greet a well-loved owner in a friendly and confident invitation that is sure of a positive reception. Senior, confident dogs tend to reflect it in their bearing, which is usually relaxed and friendly but self-contained.

BELOW A laid-back pointer, who had settled down to nap, was woken by a slammed door. His eyes are slightly dilated and his ears are coming forward, but the relaxed mouth and calm posture show that he is taking even this rude awakening in his stride.

LEFT Like many dogs who are familiar with one another, these two inseparable Chihuahua crossbreds have developed an interaction that looks like a highly tuned and predictable dance. Very aware of each other's moves, each follows the direction of the other's gaze.

DIRECTION You sometimes see a dog's head facing in a different direction from its body. In everyday situations, when a dog is following its impulses, head and body "agree" and follow the same course. However, when the dog is anxious — perhaps when he is nervous about following through with an action he is considering, such as wanting to greet a person or dog he isn't quite sure of, or is about to step into another dog's body space to take a much-wanted toy — you will see his body facing in the direction in which he wants to go, but his head facing downwards, off to the side. His body language reads, "I'm not sure about this." It's like an extreme version of the averted-eye signal.

RIGHT A lowered head and an averted gaze, combined with braced legs and ears folded well back, tell us that this isn't a happy dog. He is uneasy, and his exposed stomach tells us that he's not offering any threat — he'd simply rather be somewhere else.

TAILS

Tails are important tools for working dogs, and they are
extensively used in other situations to convey intent. Puppies
start to use their tails when they are still very young and
gradually learn their full extent as aids to communication.
Tail language seems to be a mixture of intentional signals and
instinctive body talk, and is extensively used by every dog. How
easy it is for us to read depends a good deal on the tail type.

Strongly curved tails like this husky's may be hard to read; their movements are relatively small.

This Pekingese has a curved tail, carried high.

Easy to read, a broad-based tail belonging to a dalmatian.

RIGHT Don't invariably read a tail carried low as a sign of stress or discomfort. This greyhound wears his tail low naturally, as do many other hounds.

A "wolf" tail: thickly furred, like that of primitive dog types.

A strong, heavily feathered tail belonging to a Chinese crested.

A balanced, well-fringed tail carried low.

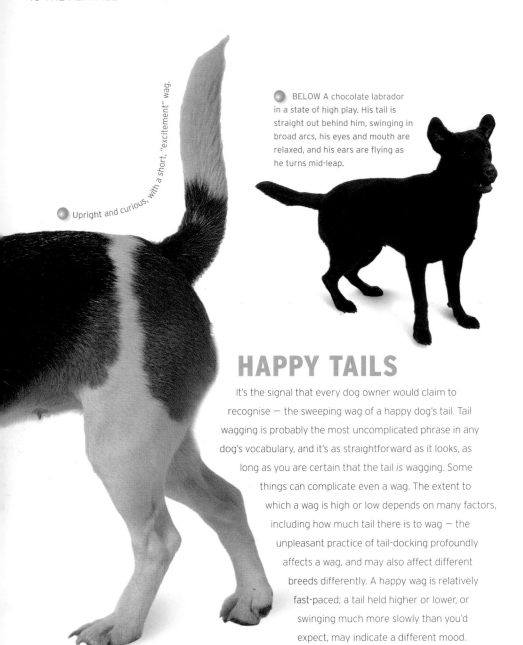

Upright and curious, with a short, "excitement" wag.

BELOW A chocolate labrador in a state of high play. His tail is straight out behind him, swinging in broad arcs, his eyes and mouth are relaxed, and his ears are flying as he turns mid-leap.

HAPPY TAILS

It's the signal that every dog owner would claim to recognise — the sweeping wag of a happy dog's tail. Tail wagging is probably the most uncomplicated phrase in any dog's vocabulary, and it's as straightforward as it looks, as long as you are certain that the tail *is* wagging. Some things can complicate even a wag. The extent to which a wag is high or low depends on many factors, including how much tail there is to wag — the unpleasant practice of tail-docking profoundly affects a wag, and may also affect different breeds differently. A happy wag is relatively fast-paced; a tail held higher or lower, or swinging much more slowly than you'd expect, may indicate a different mood.

DIFFERENT WAG = DIFFERENT MESSAGE If a

broad sweep represents a happy greeting, the wag you see most
often when a dog is playing is a slightly slower movement — a
gentle wave. A higher tail vibrating in short, sharp bursts may be
warning you off — for example, if a dog is feeling possessive over
a toy. Look at what the rest of the body is telling you to confirm
the message. In play, you will see a whole gamut of tail talk, and
you can watch the changes in tail position and movement in
context. When a high-tension chase-and-pounce is going on, the
tail may be held completely still for a second before the body
direction changes and the dog plunges back in at full pelt.

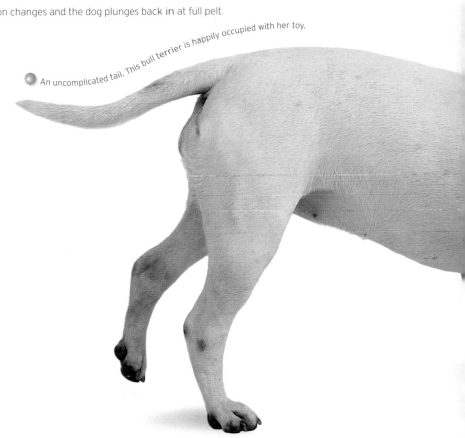

An uncomplicated tail. This bull terrier is happily occupied with her toy.

NEUTRAL INTO ACTION

Dogs spend a lot of time simply holding their tails still. When they are peaceful and nothing in particular is going on, this stillness is neutral; but there are also moments of alert stillness, when a dog has noticed and become interested in something, but hasn't yet decided what action to take. You see these "frozen" moments in pairs of dogs who have completed the preliminaries and are just about to launch into a game, and in dogs who are unhappy about a situation and are considering whether to withdraw or engage in less friendly activity. Changes in posture indicate a changing focus, and other dogs can read and respond to the nuances. Relatively few moments of stillness spell trouble, but for an owner, learning to read them accurately can be both revealing of your dog's character and useful in defusing problem situations.

● ABOVE This little Chihuahua is watching a toy held by his owner. His body is still, but leaning up as he strains towards the coveted object; his tail is raised, ready to move into a full wag as he's given the toy.

● BELOW This beagle/basset cross is mid-game but her owner has produced a treat. Her tail is moving in broad arcs as her attention focuses.

Expressive tails may be good indicators of the level of a dog's excitement, but sometimes less clearly (to humans at least) of its nature. When naturalists first began to attempt a real interpretation of dog talk, the broadly accepted "rule" was that the higher a dog's tail was being held, the more confident the posture, and that a tail carried low was a sign of "submission" within the pack hierarchy. But observation will tell you that a high tail may indicate a state of happy excitement or aggression, and a low tail can be showing a momentary "making my mind up" state as well as fear or discomfort. As always, it's best to learn the signs one by one and then read the whole dog for a good picture of what's really going on — the tail is an important piece of the jigsaw, but it doesn't tell the whole story.

BELOW Distracted by another dog, she turns, but her tail is still swinging in a broad, steady arc and her body language remains relaxed and friendly. Hound tails like this are often carried relatively low except when the dog is very excited.

◐ TAILS IN CONTEXT

This dog's mood has gone a stage beyond discomfort; adding up all the signals you can see here, he's feeling fearful. Dogs are sometimes more upset than we expect them to be by apparently ordinary circumstances — but then, they know what they are disconcerted by and we don't. In this case, the combination of a confined and enclosed space and a brief fracas with an unfamiliar dog pushed this sheepdog into high stress, and he is sending clear signals of just how bad he is feeling.

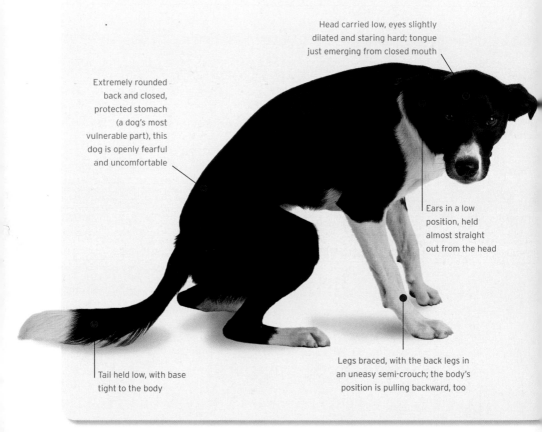

Head carried low, eyes slightly dilated and staring hard; tongue just emerging from closed mouth

Extremely rounded back and closed, protected stomach (a dog's most vulnerable part), this dog is openly fearful and uncomfortable

Ears in a low position, held almost straight out from the head

Tail held low, with base tight to the body

Legs braced, with the back legs in an uneasy semi-crouch; the body's position is pulling backward, too

Unlike the sheepdog on the left, this little dachshund is merely uncomfortable. His tolerance is at a low ebb, but he isn't really frightened. How to read his language? His ears are only slightly turned back; they are in near — but not completely — neutral; his tail is turned in, but is not dramatically clamped under him. His chin is down, and he is directing a strong look at his owner, who is standing off to the right. His brow is somewhat tensed up, resulting in a puzzled look — this is yet another sign of discomfort. Finally, the line of his back is a little rounded. Every one of these signals tells you "I don't want to be here", but there's no sign of fear. In both of these pictures, the tail signs the state of play clearly.

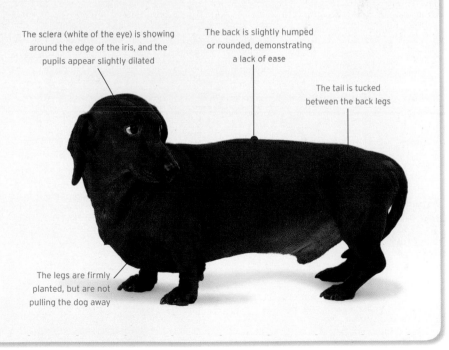

The sclera (white of the eye) is showing around the edge of the iris, and the pupils appear slightly dilated

The back is slightly humped or rounded, demonstrating a lack of ease

The tail is tucked between the back legs

The legs are firmly planted, but are not pulling the dog away

BACKS AND LEGS

You can read a lot of basic information about a dog's mood from how he or she is standing, and the shape of his or her back. Legs and paws are also used expressively, and both backs and legs are relatively easy to "read" for the onlooker; they give broad information that you can augment by looking at what the ears, mouths, tails and eyes are doing. A square, stiff stance on four braced legs is forceful, the sign of a dog that is highly reactive for one reason or another; "easier" poses, with legs placed rather than braced, are more relaxed. All three dogs here are highly animated, but all are clearly playing — and all are also behaving characteristically. The braced legs and high tail of the fox terrier tell you that he is "wired" for action, but look closer and the slight squintiness you can see at the corner of the eye tells you it's only play.

● RIGHT You can often see dogs "controlling" the pace of a game using a paw on their playmate. Here, both dogs have lifted their paws simultaneously. Although the pushier Lakeland has got his gesture in first . . .

RIGHT The stiff, braced posture of the fox terrier is entirely focused on the game of tug with his human. Stiff-legged stances can sometimes signal tension or aggression, but this dog is simply concentrating on winning back his toy.

LEFT ... this doesn't win him higher stakes in the game; within a second, the Samoyed had calmly out-pawed him. Both dogs have the open, relaxed mouths that tell you that this is still play.

TENSE BACKS

The dogs on this page are showing a range of expressions in their "toplines", the upper line of their backs. The topline is a basic way to read a dog's comfort level — a relaxed dog has an easy carriage and his back will be in a straight (but not rigid) line, like the Lakeland at lower right. At first glance, the fox terrier, below, has a similar carriage, but if you look more closely, his tail and head are both down and there is a suggestion of stiffness and a very slight rounding in his back that tell us that he isn't quite sure. A definitely rounded back, like that of the Jack Russell on the right, is sending much stronger signals of discomfort.

This fox terrier's posture suggests indecision — tail and head down, back very slightly rounded.

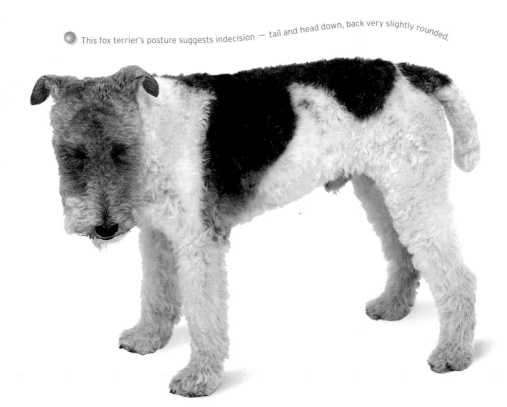

RIGHT A strongly rounded back, slightly tensed front paws, as well as an "indecisive"-looking rear end in this Jack Russell terrier all add up to a pose that suggests some apprehension.

In contrast to the other pictures, this is a completely relaxed, active pose, with no tension in the back.

WHOLE-BODY STANCE

Most of the earlier sections have concentrated on signs sent by dogs' faces and tails — either end of the body, as it were. Looking at what dogs' legs and backs are doing helps you to put the whole-body position in context and get a complete picture of what a dog is saying. Although at first you might think that both the dogs here are sitting, and both have open, relaxed mouths, the key to how switched-on their alert systems are lies in the back legs. One is crouching, fully alert and ready for action, the other, although cheerful and alert, is genuinely sitting and is on much less of a hair trigger. The bodies of dogs in high alert tend toward a more streamlined look — for example, one of the signs that a play chase between two dogs is

LEFT Dogs in a strongly reactive, "on the go" state will often assume this position: at first glance it looks like a sit, but the rear end is actually being held clear of the floor by tense, muscular back legs.

becoming serious (perhaps too serious for comfort) is that the pursuing dog will start to look as though his body has stretched and become longer. The slightly bouncy looseness characteristic of play disappears from the back and legs, and the whole body moves more intently and lower to the ground. Equally, a very still dog, if his pose is also rigid, may be moving towards forceful reaction. Other dogs notice these changes in body pose and react to them speedily. When a dog suddenly decides to depart the scene, it is often because another has begun to give off these stronger body signals and is creating a feeling of tension. The signs are quick, and the first thing you may notice is the reaction of a departing dog, but the earlier signs will have been there, even if only briefly and subtly.

LEFT The fox terrier, however, really is sitting down. Back legs are turned to one side, leaving an exposed, relaxed belly, and front legs are placed rather than braced. Despite this, his animated head, with open mouth, forward ears and alert eyes, tells us he is still ready to go.

MOUTHS AND TEETH

All dogs send signals a good deal using movements of their mouths and, on occasion, displays of their teeth. The quick movement with which a dog speedily licks his nose or the edge of his mouth (a "tongue flick") is a sign that dogs frequently make, and one that you might read as accidental unless you watch closely how and when it is used. It's one of the more ambiguous signals a dog can send, but it's often directed at another dog as part of the negotiation procedure dogs use to safely cross one another's path or enter one another's space. Almost all dogs are proprietorial about their own turf, whether that means somewhere specific, such as a basket, or is temporarily signified by a few feet of clear space in which they are standing.

BELOW This fox terrier is a confident dog, slightly undecided about the other dogs milling around the room. As he tried to play, a less confident dog snapped at him nervously; he paused momentarily, did a quick tongue flick, collected himself and went back to the group.

LEFT These two pointers have been asked to "stay". One promptly sat down; the other is performing a quick tongue flick directly at his owner — he's not certain what he's supposed to be doing or why he's here. He's looking at her for some additional information about the situation.

If you watch a group of dogs moving about in a relatively confined area, you will see tongue flicks used frequently, sometimes combined with other signals. The message is that the dog does not have all the information it needs to move about freely, and can signal discomfort with a set of unfamiliar circumstances. The longer you watch, the more obvious it becomes that these signs are deliberately directed at another dog or a person; they are rarely made to an empty space. The Lakeland puppy on the right, for example, was just passing uncomfortably close to a larger, older dog en route to a toy he wanted to fetch — but he is clearly telling the senior dog that he has no pretensions. Even the little fox terrier on the left, who had temporarily left the arena, was directing his signal in the direction of the dog who had just snapped at him, although he was apparently also using this slightly separate place to calm himself, too.

BELOW This terrier is in some stress, and he's using several signals: lowered head, braced legs, rounded back, plus a quick, nervous tongue flick.

 LEFT This Samoyed had played amiably and enthusiastically with a number of other dogs, but gradually he began to display symptoms of tiredness and slight overload. Eventually, the Samoyed lay down, facing at a right angle to the others, and yawned so that they could see him. Apparently he was giving everyone notice that he was leaving the play arena.

YAWNING

Just like us, dogs yawn when tired — yawning is the body's way of getting more oxygen to a tired system fast — but they also yawn when they are stressed or confused. What might be called tactical yawning is seen most either when a dog is making it clear that he or she is not involved in a group situation or when a dog is extricating himself from a mildly tense meeting or a minor confrontation with another. Yawning deflects interest, it makes it clear that the dog is not a player in whatever drama is going on, and it underlines to others that he is engaged in something else. It seems to be used more by dogs who are standing back, or who want to stand back, than those who are trying to negotiate with other dogs about the outcome of a situation, and, therefore, it falls into the category of calming signals — sent by dogs with the aim of defusing tension by giving other dogs clear information. Non-tactical yawning seems to happen most when a dog is trying to make himself comfortable in an unfamiliar situation or space in which he is not sure of the status quo.

ABOVE This fox terrier was watching some tense manoeuvring between two relatively senior dogs when he sat down and yawned in their direction. The message seemed to be, "I'm no part of this; I'm staying out of it." The sitting in itself may have been intended as a "stop" signal to the other dogs. As soon as an exit route opened for him he left the room altogether.

RELAXED MOUTHS

In general, dogs close their mouths when in a tense situation; relaxed, happy dogs have their mouths open, often with a bit of tongue lolling out. The Samoyed and the collie on these pages both have typically relaxed faces, although neither dog is in neutral mode — both are considering a situation and deciding what to do about it. If a dog is making a friendly advance to someone else — canine or human — these are typical expressions. If a meeting with another dog looks as if it is going to extend into a game, the initiating dog will often open and close his mouth several times before he goes into a "play bow" to tempt the other into a chase.

● ABOVE Treats are being given by an owner to her dogs to the left of this Samoyed. She's a confident dog, but still pauses as she considers if it's an inclusive situation. We can see that she is relaxed from her poised stance, forward ears, cheerfully "up" tail and, most of all, from her happy, loose face — there is no tension at all around her mouth.

DEVELOPING SITUATIONS If you watch a dog through a series of events, from a neutral position to an active role — meeting another dog, starting a game or negotiating his way through a disagreement — you will see him opening and shutting his mouth a lot. Even in a relaxed scenario where the dog is happy with what is happening, he will usually close his mouth quickly as though he were "punctuating" his demeanour, at each point when things change.

LEFT Waiting for instruction, this sheepdog is focusing on his trainer in the middle of an exercise; the open mouth with slightly lolling tongue and relaxed muzzle tell us that he is happy, familiar and trusting of the situation.

"WHAT'S GOING ON?"

This Lakeland terrier is showing interest in a developing situation. His mouth has closed a little from its neutral open position, his "lips" are blown out a little in anticipation, his eyes are slightly rounded, and his face shows a slight tightening up. This isn't intense body language — it's a pose you'll see a dog holding momentarily dozens of times a day. It's casual interest in a slight stimulus; a change from passive observer to an onlooker who may get active.

LEFT This dog displays some idiosyncratic behaviour. When her owner paid too much attention to another dog in the room, she rushed over to them with an alarming expression, showing plenty of teeth. As she reached the offending pair she ignored the other dog, instead making a big fuss of her owner. In retrospect, this seemed to be her "stop!" face; despite the wildly rolling eye, the curled (not tense) upper lip is a clue that the threat is not serious. It was, rather, a histrionic warning.

TENSE MOUTHS

When is a snarl not a snarl? It can be hard to tell (and it's best to go cautiously) unless you know the dog well, but there are always clues. Despite their intimidating displays of teeth, neither of the dogs here is in a state of high aggression. The Samoyed on the left is rushing to claim what's hers — her owner's attention — while the dog below is simply sounding off at the slow appearance of an expected treat. The Samoyed's position is odd because of her high-raised nose. The posture looks primitive, like a howling wolf. Nonetheless, when she reached her owner, she didn't even warn off the "threatening" dog who was claiming all the attention: she simply worked at getting the focus back on herself with a display of licking and jumping, using puppy-like, deferential behaviour.

The Jack Russell is a simpler story. This dog doesn't like waiting for anything; in the ten seconds during which she was waiting for a reward, she started screwing up her nose, showing her teeth and making small grunting noises to signify her impatience. Both dogs are displaying mouths that look fierce, but the curled upper lip is usually used only with familiar recipients, and neither is in a truly tense situation.

LEFT Lots of teeth, but this Jack Russell is demanding a treat, displaying impatience in true terrier fashion.

VOCALISATION

The majority of dogs' language is expressed through body signs and signals instead of noise. At close range, or face-to-face, small-scale, subtle signing (a tongue flick, an ear swivel, a lowered tail and so on) serves for most casual, everyday situations. Although dogs can make a wide range of sounds, you may hear few of them in the course of ordinary shared human/canine life. A visit to the park and a half-hour or so spent observing groups of dogs interacting will offer vignettes of most of the other signs and signals in *Tail Talk*, and will probably yield more barking than you would hear at home, but there is a rich repertoire of canine vocals that is used more rarely. While some dogs bark a lot, and make a wide range of other noises, others are naturally quiet and you will rarely hear them "speak" at all. Originally wild dogs judged when to use sound. Noises to communicate usually aren't good when hunting, for example — that would mean exerting your breath and alerting your quarry. Over time, dogs learned to use sounds only when they were useful.

LEFT This dog is "singing" to music as a party trick. He was never particularly encouraged to do so — in fact, he started to perform naturally. Some researchers into animal behaviour believe that when dogs join in, adding their noise to a sound that is already happening, they are instinctively adding their own note to a group initiative.

This dalmatian is emitting a constant low whine. She's trying to get her owner to play with her.

INDULGENT SOUNDS

Dog owners are sometimes surprised by the sounds dogs make when they are deeply contented. The owner of this elderly Lakeland described his happy noise as a "purr" — a low, melodious, grumbling sound more reminiscent of a cat than a dog. Another dog "growled" as an inducement to her owner to carry on with a belly rub. Highly individual, only dogs who are relaxed and feel no threat to their well-being make these sounds.

PITCH AND VOLUME

Just as with their body language, dogs may use sound in two separate ways: deliberately to communicate a message or involuntarily as an expression of how they are feeling. The fox terrier shown below wanted to play a game with an older dog (not shown) and was doing both simultaneously. He could no longer conceal his impatience, so the noise he was making seemed almost involuntary; but at the same time, he was effectively communicating his urgency to the older dog. The noise seemed to be used as a last resort — he had already run through a whole gamut of play bows and excited pounces before launching into a high, repetitive yipping that was gradually raised, both in volume and in pitch. (It worked — he was finally rewarded with a game.) Key to the noise this terrier made was its pitch.

BELOW This fox terrier is a naturally vocal dog, who always makes a lot of noise whether playing or in earnest. Playing one of his frequent games of tug, he "talks" in a low, grumbling tone, steady in volume, but variable in pitch and tone.

As a very general rule, high-pitched sounds indicate excitement but without threat; the lower the pitch of the sound a dog makes, the more careful you should be. High barks, whines and squeaks don't sound threatening but, as with humans, the lower the pitch at which a noise is made, the more seriously we take it. A person speaking low expects to be taken seriously; usually, too, the slower he speaks, the more seriously he intends to be taken. Dogs broadly operate by the same rule — the most threatening sounds (deep snarls, low growls) are also pitched the lowest. Puppies approached by an adult of whom they are not certain will make high-pitched whimpering sounds, sending the message that they pose no threat, and an adult dog under threat may make the same noise.

The volume of sound says nothing about social status. Volume seems to depend much more on the character and breeding of the particular dog who is making it.

BELOW How can you tell this terrier's play talk from a real growl? To the human ear it often sounds fierce enough. If you hear a real, aggressive growl, though, it's easy to tell the difference. A dog who intends the warning to be taken seriously tends to start the low, menacing noise at one pitch and keep going without change. If he needs to, he will draw breath and start again, but the noise he's making will be on a single note. And, usually, the lower the pitch, the more serious the warning.

RIGHT These two terriers loathed one another on sight. Each sent a range of signals warning the other to keep out of their body space — and the fact that they were both leashed made the situation more difficult for them. When the signs were ignored, both launched into a barrage of snarling and barking. All the noise was warning, though — mouths remained wide open, and, despite some opportunity, there was no contact biting.

TYPES OF SOUND

If you consider the range of sounds a dog can potentially make — barking, howling, yipping and squeaking, plus a wide gamut of groans, sighs and snorts — you may wonder why you hear such a limited range from your own dog. This may have as much to do with your pet's breed history as it has to do with the animal himself or herself. The "barkier" dogs tend to be those that needed to communicate with each other over distances — for example, beagles or harriers working a fox as a group, or terriers going to ground when hunting. Barking is a useful distance signal to alert others if you are working as a team. However, barking doesn't have much function in many guarding or herding activities. Researchers have postulated that the closer to a wild dog a breed is, the more likely it is to howl — like a wolf. Dogs are still instinctive in many things, but don't underestimate the extent to which their signals have come to fit in with human behaviour during the long process of their domestication.

◓ WARNING NOISES

All the deliberate, communicative warning noises that dogs make are just that — warnings. Once a dog has decided that negotiation conducted with body language and noises is useless, he will go into action. That's why it's so important that you pay attention to aggressive noises. In the lower ranges, a growl can be difficult to hear, yet the lowest growl, a constant, level noise, is probably the one most likely to precipitate action.

EXCITED NOISES

Because humans communicate through speech more than by any other means, some dogs have learned to communicate directly with us by means of noise instead of — or in addition to — the body language that they might be inclined to use more exclusively with their own species. Most owners are used to being encouraged, or nagged, towards a walk or a game; some dogs will bark to send a message that it's dinner time, as well as, more instinctively, to let us know that strangers are approaching or there's someone at the front door. Noises and body language are often intermingled in dog-to-dog relations. Barking is the noise we most

LEFT Lots of teeth plus a big dose of rapid-fire barking is this Jack Russell's play-talk. Terriers were bred to make plenty of noise so that they could be located while hunting underground or underbrush.

commonly hear, and there are 10 or 12 gradations in barks to the human ear alone. Listen to a group of dogs and see how many you can hear, from the clear, excited "ruff!" that moves on to a higher note as it is repeated (often used as a call to playmates to rejoin a game) to the single, sharp bark that can signify a warning to someone who has overstepped the boundaries. Because humans are most used to sound communication, it may be easier for you to hear the gradations in a noise at first than to distinguish the finer points of often complex body language.

BELOW Play-growling can sound just like the real thing — this Samoyed is fully focused on her tug toy, and is making a strong, fierce sound. Her ears are back, too, and the whites of her eyes are showing — were she staring at the person, rather than the toy, this would be a definite threat. One sign that this is all a game is the slight paw lift.

THE PHRASE BOOK

WATCH THE HOUND

When a dog is interacting with others, you should watch the whole group to form an accurate idea of what's going on. If you concentrate on one dog and exclude the others, it's like hearing just one side of a conversation.

Not only will you see a lot of signs in the Phrase Book that are already familiar from the Alphabet section, but as you see the same dogs reappearing in different situations you'll also begin to get an idea of how canine personalities affect body language. The pushy male fox terrier, for example, elicits different reactions from the confident young retriever bitch and the serious male boxer dog, while dogs who are meeting for the first time are often easily distinguished from those who are old friends or companions by the signs they send. In the following pages, the context is described alongside the pictures, giving you a three-dimensional insight into what's going on.

LEFT AND BELOW These three Chihuahuas are used to one another, but not to the setting. The two on the right confidently respond (below) to the offer of a treat. The one on the left, though, is uneasy and wants to leave; see how her pinned-back ears and rounded back in the first picture quickly translate to a low-body escape attempt in the second.

SAME POSE, DIFFERENT REASONS

Whenever a dog rolls on his or her back, it is exposing itself
to risk — it's the most helpless position a dog can adopt and
therefore the most deferential and open to interaction. A dog
will use this pose in a range of different circumstances. In the
first picture, the retriever puppy (a self-possessed eight-month-
old) is looking for attention from her owner. She approached him,
wagging gently, looked directly at him and then rolled over in a
clear demonstration of friendly solicitation, hoping to interact.
When she was ignored for a few seconds she started to wriggle,
wave her paws in the air and wag her tail, writhing from side to
side and "smiling" with a wide-open mouth. She wanted a belly
rub; she was actually making a request, although from a classic
submissive posture. In the second picture the puppy had met the
boxer for the first time five minutes before, and after an initial

ABOVE Waiting for a belly
rub from her owner, this young
retriever is completely relaxed,
wriggling from side to side and
arching her back.

bout of relatively modest rear-sniffing, it became clear that the boxer was determined to establish more about her. She immediately rolled into a pose that was less engaged, but clearly deferential, giving him full access. In this picture, she is lying still, mouth closed, paws "frozen". She isn't frightened, but she is slightly tense. Having learned as much as he was going to, the boxer "allowed" her up, and they started to play chase.

BELOW The same dog is sending a different message. This time, the younger bitch is allowing an examination from an older male boxer. She's remaining still and letting him assure himself that she's not posing any threat to his status.

CALMING AND DEFERENTIAL

When two strange dogs meet in the park, how often have you heard their embarrassed owners say, "Why does she *always* have to *do* that?" They're referring to the rear-sniffing (or genital sniffing) with which dogs introduce themselves. With a sense of smell more than forty times as strong as ours, dogs can get more information from the back end of a dog than the front (although, as the exchange here shows, they will often sniff around noses and mouths, too). Looking on, you can tell a lot about a dog's confidence levels. In this exchange, both dogs are friendly. The Samoyed is confident; the Lakeland is a little more wired and excited (look at those ears and that raised back leg).

ABOVE This young Lakeland terrier is excitable and forward. Here, he is meeting a friendly older Samoyed for the first time. The open lips and relaxed mouth of the older dog make it clear that there is no threat here. The two dogs start with a face-to-face sniff.

The older Samoyed sniffs the terrier puppy first and decides that he is friendly.

ABOVE Finally, the Lakeland reciprocates by sniffing the older dog. This calm, friendly exchange tells both dogs what they need to know about one another.

INITIATING PLAY

Here, the Lakeland puppy considered how he could start a game with the senior dog. He tried a couple of bouncy play bows (backside in air, head down); when they did not succeed, he sat down for a moment, then raced around the Samoyed, barging into her from the side. The Samoyed was not going to be hustled, although she was happy to get involved. She positioned herself over the puppy, ensuring that he was aware of her relative size and height. Then she nudged him over with her head and paws, and started to play as he rolled around on his back.

What's striking about this exchange is its good humour. The younger, pushier dog is reminded of his position calmly and agreeably. Had he tried the same tactic with a less confident dog, it's unlikely that it would have met with such a kind reception.

BELOW Having completed introductions, the Lakeland lies down for a minute. Dogs sometimes have a moment's stillness before initiating a play chase, and this seems to be what he had in mind. Ears forward, mouth open and braced paws are all showing strong interest; he isn't still for long.

LEFT When the Samoyed did not immediately respond to a play bow, the terrier moves in, barging into her slightly. By standing over the puppy, the Samoyed exerts some semblance of control.

Playing is an important exchange for most dogs — and most, although not all, love to play. It can act as a harmless trial of strength and as a way to get to know each other and each other's responses. Watching dogs play, you will be aware of the constant exchange of signals and body language. In the picture at the top of this page, the Lakeland paused momentarily as the Samoyed moved into his body space, appearing to jostle a little to regain her control of the situation. Then both dogs sprang back into motion as the Samoyed pounced. Having rolled the terrier over, it was her turn to pause as he absorbed what had happened. When play resumed, although both dogs were fully participating, the small terrier was showing more deference to the larger, older dog.

ABOVE She then rolls him over, but gently. Both dogs are enjoying this, but it's definitely the Samoyed who is setting the pace.

STARTING A CONVERSATION

When dogs first meet they send a lot of signals quickly about who they are and what they expect. Neither of the two dogs here is confident: the fox terrier tends to alternate between pushiness and uncertainty, and the boxer is a reserved dog who doesn't always get along with others. On first meeting they exchanged a perfunctory rear-sniff, then moved at right angles, head to head. For a moment they appeared to be jousting, each laying his head over the other's neck, in one version of a canine "stop" signal. The boxer seemed to "win", as the fox terrier suddenly moved out of his body space, expressing slight discomfort (rounded back, tail held still) and began to sniff the ground. The boxer followed, and performed another rear-sniff. The fox terrier's apparent backdown calmed the tension — they didn't play, but the dogs seemed subsequently content to share the limited space.

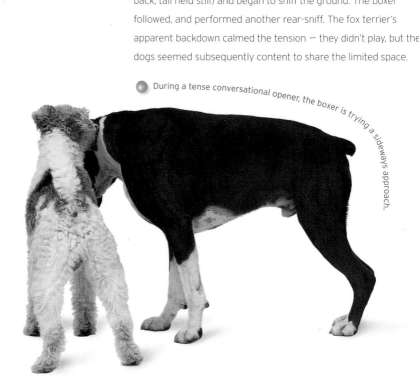

During a tense conversational opener, the boxer is trying a sideways approach.

BELOW Neither dog is relaxed (note the boxer's rounded back and braced legs) in this uneasy truce. The fox terrier decides that discretion is the better part of valour and departs.

BELOW The fox terrier starts to sniff the ground — this may signify "I'm engaged with something else; I'm not threatening you." Emboldened, the boxer moves in for a rear-sniff. The language of both dogs is cautious.

DEFLECTING ACTION

Dogs have a wide range of signs to choose from to signify that they don't want to be involved. It can be hard to distinguish this behaviour and divide it into component parts — some signs may be displacement activities and part of the dog's genetic predisposition, while others may serve the function of calming signals to other dogs. Some may simultaneously calm the dog himself and persuade those around him that he poses no threat. Displacement activities are often seen when a dog is in an unfamiliar place and is feeling uncomfortable. Sniffing the ground, sudden keen self-grooming (hard licking, biting or scratching of the paws or other parts of the body) or yawning can all play this role; equally, they can be used to convey to other dogs that this dog isn't intending to get involved in what is going on around him.

ABOVE Although calm in one-to-one situations with other dogs, this Samoyed is less comfortable with groups of several dogs. Confronted with four other dogs simultaneously, she retreated to a corner and started an emphatic sniffing routine. She made no eye contact with the other dogs; otherwise, her body language was calm and reflective.

CALLING TIME

Some dogs use "time out" signals when they want a break. This retriever puppy seemed suddenly overwhelmed by being the centre of an attentive group. Withdrawing to its edge, she first sat, then lay down and spent a few moments scratching, and grooming her paws, then returned to the fray. Was it a "real" itch? Probably not — she was avoiding eye contact with the other players.

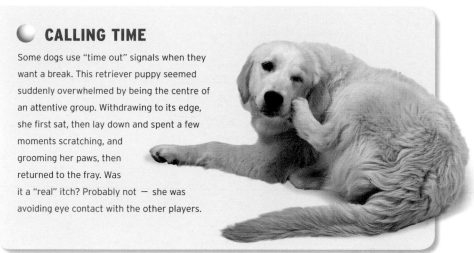

BELOW After sniffing for a minute or two, the Samoyed began a thorough paw-wash. She continued to be completely engaged until most of the other dogs left the space.

The collie crossbreed is evidently uncomfortable with the fox terrier's enthusiastic introduction.

SIGNALLING NERVES

Sometimes a dog just knows it doesn't want to be where it finds itself. The encounter shown here is unambiguous. This collie crossbreed bitch — usually a confident, outgoing character — was upset by the close quarters. Out of doors, in an unconfined area, she would not have hesitated to correct the fox terrier's presumptuous approach very harshly; indoors, in the unfamiliar space, she was only thinking of the quickest route to the exit. Her splayed, braced legs, lowered head, closed mouth and rounded back are all conveying her discomfort. She dodged about for a moment, then made her way past the fox terrier (who was characteristically impervious to the signals she was sending) and went straight to her owner.

FEELING CORNERED When pet dogs meet for the first time, the introduction will usually go smoothly provided that there is plenty of space and room to get away if the introduction isn't comfortable. Dogs will usually feel most comfortable meeting dogs that are new to them with lots of room — out of doors, in open ground. Other factors that can provoke some confrontational behaviour are anything — a rope toy, a ball — over which one dog may feel proprietorial. Serious quarrels between dogs are often the result of one or the other of the protagonists feeling trapped and not seeing an exit route. If there is enough room for everyone to maintain their personal space, dogs usually sort themselves out quickly by means of mutually recognised signs. As soon as the boundaries have been established, the social situation will settle down fast.

BELOW Beating a retreat, the collie cross has had enough. Everything about her body language suggests a dog who is really intimidated — too many unfamiliar elements at the same time have proved to be overwhelming.

BELOW Probably the only signal that is as universally recognised as a simple tail wag, the play bow, with paws on ground and rear up, looks similar whatever the shape, age or breed.

HAPPY AND RELAXED

The play bow makes an appearance in most games between dogs. The picture below shows a textbook example — forelegs flat on the ground and rear raised. Combined with a relaxed face, open mouth and wagging tail, this constitutes an almost irresistible invitation to play. Playful dogs will often send this sign within a minute or two of being introduced. When dogs are playing intensely, you will also see this pose used to create a pause in the game, often after passages of particularly frantic paw wrestling or chasing. Sometimes it appears to be used as a deliberate sign to calm things down — if one dog forgets himself and begins to play with uncomfortable intensity, another may pause and go into a play bow to remind him that this isn't serious.

Both dogs pause momentarily — the mutual play bow is a signal for the chaser to become the chased, and vice versa.

○ PLAYFUL OR SERIOUS?

As with human communication, there are plenty of exceptions and eccentricities in dog talk. This boxer often looks uncertain about joining a game; however, he's a keen chaser, and dogs who know him launch straight in. His body language here isn't encouraging, yet seconds after the picture was taken he was happily "fast chasing". New dogs treat him with caution, so evidently his body language is a little enigmatic, even to other dogs.

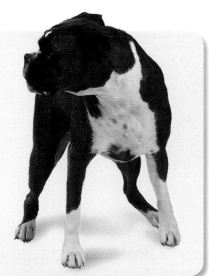

THE RULES
OF THE GAME

Existing relationships may be modified when dogs play, and a dog who might otherwise feel he should be taking the lead may periodically relinquish it during a game. Although the bull terrier and basset/beagle crossbreed in these pictures are good friends, the bull terrier takes the leading role and usually has final say. In play, however, she knows it's less enjoyable if she always wins.

The solution both dogs have found is that the bull terrier has the toy for most of the time in the course of any game, but the basset always has the chance of winning it back — and gets it often enough to make the game worthwhile for her, too. The basset offers the bull terrier plenty of negotiating signs whenever she makes a bid for the toy, while the bull terrier reins back her forcefulness sufficiently to keep things exciting for both dogs. All this is achieved with fluent, fast body language, enjoyable to watch. The end of the game is always signified by the bull terrier taking the toy more forcefully and leaving the scene with it. In the final move, she makes it plain that she calls the shots.

BELOW The squeaky toy has already been exchanged several times. The bull terrier usually ends up with the toy. The basset crossbreed is heading off quickly, seeking to evade capture a little longer.

◑ HUMAN INVITATIONS

Dogs invite people to play, too. You will often
see a play bow offered to a human companion,
and some dogs will also learn to "ask" for a
game — we're all familiar with the dog who
perpetually fetches his ball or squeaky toy and
repeatedly drops it at our feet. This Samoyed
has not been trained to "paw lift" as an
invitation to her owner to play — she's simply
discovered that it's the most effective way
to get a reaction.

◑ BELOW Sure enough, the bull terrier has won the toy
back. However, she doesn't want the game to stop, so she
stands still. The basset crossbreed is getting ready for a
pounce. Note the lowered front body, high tail and quick
tongue flick — she's giving the bull terrier advance warning.

The mouthy Lakeland is trying a tooth-display ploy on the Samoyed, who is firmly pulling back. The puppy is trying to start a game.

MOUTH WRESTLING

Dogs show their teeth a lot in play, but rarely with aggressive intent. A pair of dogs may hold their jaws wide to engage in "mouth wrestling", but if you watch their play sequence closely, you will see that their teeth are usually covered by their lips and that they are careful never to actually close them on the skin of the other dog. Puppies mouth things continually — where a human baby might feel things with its hands, a puppy will try something with its mouth. Once dogs are adults, this mouthing may continue both in active play and to act as a comforter when a dog is alone. Many grown dogs favour soft toys that they mouth and that apparently serve a function similar to a comfort blanket. This is a habit practised by both males and females, and the toys do not appear to be surrogate puppies. The tooth display in the picture on the right was not a prelude to play — instead, it seemed to be an intimate routine of "tooth grooming" between close friends.

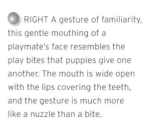

RIGHT A gesture of familiarity, this gentle mouthing of a playmate's face resembles the play bites that puppies give one another. The mouth is wide open with the lips covering the teeth, and the gesture is much more like a nuzzle than a bite.

RIGHT The bait is still not being taken, and now the Lakeland, increasingly frantic for a game, is really pushing his luck. The Samoyed is angling her body away from him as sharply as she can; she's a gentle dog and will only rebuke the puppy if he really oversteps the limits.

SHARING

Sometimes, when play goes wrong and becomes overly aggressive, human onlookers will claim that the conflict "came out of nowhere". This is hardly ever true — all that it usually means is that either the signs were too subtle or that they happened too fast for the human eye to see. Never forget that dogs are complex, territorial animals just like any other social mammal, humans included. However happy they may be to lay on the couch with you, it doesn't mean that their old animal instincts are dormant — just that they choose not to display them when there isn't a need.

BELOW Evenly matched dogs playing tug. Although there is no tension in either dog's body language, the black-and-white pointer appears to be taking the game quite seriously, judging by her direct stare.

Play between dogs demands constant compromise, and plenty of reinforcing body language stressing that what is happening *is* play. As you watch you will see an ever-changing reciprocal arrangement. Dogs ask questions with their body language, and act on the information they get back — and one dog will be much quicker to notice inappropriate behaviour in another than a human will. If a dog is showing anxiety even as it plays, the body language of his playmate may be worrying him in some way, and the game could be headed for trouble.

MIRRORING

As the name suggests, mirroring reflects body language that is close or identical in more than one dog. You see it when dogs are familiar with one another and are used to constant interaction. In play, each dog seems almost to anticipate the other's actions, and both dogs will show a similar response to various stimuli. This is body language that has developed over time. The bull terrier and the basset hound crossbreed on these pages duplicate each other's postures. So do the Samoyed pair above and the two pointers that look so relaxed on pages 96–97. In cases where two dogs live together, one usually plays the role of lead dog, but in none of these cases did this fact affect their duplicating action. On the right, the basset crossbreed is barging into the bull terrier in play.

ABOVE These Samoyeds with nearly identical postures live together. Their "matching" body language may be because they are naturally "simpatico" or this type of behaviour may have evolved over time.

RIGHT At the start of a play sequence, the dogs' signing is still in key. Note the double slight paw lift, the set-back ears and the politely averted gaze.

LEFT These dogs also live together. As they move around the room, the familiarity they have with one another is evident in their similar body language.

The right-angled approach immediately tells us that this isn't a serious attack (dogs with more aggressive intentions meet face-to-face, rather than sideways on). But, beyond this, look at how perfectly matched the two dogs are. Introduce the mirroring dogs into a larger group, however, and they won't necessarily stay together in the same play pattern. In a bigger group, these two will move out and interact with different dogs, and may also play singly with a new acquaintance. Their familiarity is not exclusive, and it is likely that their relationship is so comfortable because it is based on proximity and familiarity rather than on the more human interpretations of affection or loyalty we might impose on their behaviour.

RIGHT This pair had been turning in increasingly tight circles for a few minutes; a moment after this picture was taken, the bull terrier went into a play bow and initiated a chase.

CHASING

Canine games often revolve around high-speed chasing, and involve rapid and minute exchanges of signals to indicate who will be the chaser and who will be chased. Dogs use constant reminders to indicate to one another that this is play, because chasing is a part of naturally predatory behaviour, and no dog wants to be the one being chased if a game gets out of hand — particularly if it's a game involving several dogs. You will see broadly sweeping tails, open mouths and paw lifts during the chase, and the game will be punctuated by brief breaks for the participants to swap roles. Signs that a dog is beginning to take the chase too seriously include a lowered "pointed" head and body, being too focused on the dog being chased, an overly intent look (playing dogs blink and break eye contact) and a rigid, still tail. Only a real distraction, such as a loud noise, will break the chase once it has reached this point — but if something does break it, both dogs will quickly regain their poise.

● LEFT The Lakeland terrier is running in mid-chase; the Samoyed is about to turn and pause — signalling a break in the chase before it recommences. Her body is braced as she turns, and her paw is raised. Both are fully engaged in the game.

CHILLING OUT

There's no set position dogs choose to sleep in. Wild dogs usually curl up to rest — both for warmth and because it leaves them less exposed as they sleep — but domestic dogs don't always follow this pattern. Many seem to rest most comfortably stretched out fully on one side, like the two shown below. Dogs won't sleep in an uneasy situation, and they won't usually rest if they are in the presence of another dog who makes them uncomfortable. If a situation is tense, however, one dog may lie down as a calming signal to another. A full stretch, such as the one shown on the facing page, is sometimes used as a sign to another dog signifying, "I'm fully engaged in stretching here; I'm not even noticing you." There are no signs being exchanged between the duo below — while they're not actually asleep, they are as relaxed with the situation and with each other as it is possible to be.

BELOW These pointers grew up together in the same home. They've played for a while; now they're relaxing. The intimate mirrored position shows that they're completely comfortable in one another's company.

LEFT This complete stretch is usually seen when a dog is waking up, or moving from rest to activity. Some dogs will visibly and deliberately stretch each part of their body; only when the routine is finished will they get moving.

ASSERTIVE
AND AGGRESSIVE

Mine, mine, mine! Dogs say it a great deal, whether they're talking about their cushion, their bone, their toy or, not infrequently, their owner. However, there are a number of different ways to say it. The two dogs above are having an enjoyable tussle over a toy. There isn't really any tension; the game depends on one dog having the toy, then the other. If the German pointer really wanted to have the toy all to herself, she would take it off in a

ABOVE This toy is destined to be passed from dog to dog a few more times before the game is over. The pointer isn't guarding it aggressively — she's holding it by one end at just the right angle for her friend to make a successful snatch.

corner and guard it more forcefully — here, however, she is actually tempting her friend to make a grab for it. The bull terrier below is feeling genuinely possessive about the toy. Right now she doesn't feel like sharing. Instead of carrying the toy high, provoking a grab, she's holding it low and twisting her neck to avoid her friend's attempts at snatching. If a dog is really serious about guarding, it's unwise to disrupt him. If he's standing still over the object of desire, holding his tail up and waving it slowly while maintaining a steady stare, it's best to leave him alone.

BELOW The toy has been passed back and forth once or twice, but now the bull terrier really wants to get it and to keep it.

RIGHT The play is becoming more intense. The bull terrier's determination is clear, and the basset crossbreed is trying a more serious grip — on the ear — to see if she can get the toy back.

THREAT AWARENESS

Dogs are good at defusing situations without any human intervention — if you watch a group in the park you'll usually be able to pick out different personality types playing without serious disagreement. In both of the situations shown, there is a confident dog who will play the leading part in settling things down — and in neither case is it the overbearing fox terrier. The retriever is young, but very self-assured. She knows that it's best to be deferential if things get tense. She also knows that a short, sharp warning is effective if deference doesn't work. She judges her responses nicely, and they keep her out of trouble. The Jack Russell is more of an endurance type. He knows that in some cases, ignoring a situation takes the tension down a notch or two.

ABOVE When the play got too rough for the young retriever, she tried to calm things by sitting down. However, the fox terrier is a particularly thick-skinned dog, and isn't easily deterred. His response was to try to mount her . . .

⬤ EYE CONTACT

These dogs disliked each other on sight, but are reacting very differently. The fox terrier is using a hard, level stare, which is challenging and quite aggressive. The ears and braced paws stress his discomfort. The Jack Russell is trying the "I can't even see you" approach: although his face is focused on his owner, his body is leaning away from the other dog. The dogs are dealing with their discomfort passively, but they are equally uncomfortable.

⬤ LEFT . . . and he found that he had gone too far. The retriever isn't showing aggression here, but this is a firm, fast warning. She's pulled her lips back from her gums, briefly giving a good show of teeth, and there's tension in her face. The fox terrier is showing surprise, but not alarm.

NEGOTIATION

A dog's life is lived by means of negotiation. The other option open to him would be much tougher — to try to work out the things that are important to him by force. Dogs usually use their intelligence ahead of their muscle and weave their way through complex situations by breaking them down into small parts and establishing an appropriate reaction for each, both gleaning and, where necessary, asking for as much information as they can along the way to ensure that their choices are good ones. Most dogs have impressively good judgement and will choose a signal designed to calm things down rather than to raise the tension. In the vast majority of cases, a dog will correctly read a sign sent to it by another dog, and react accordingly.

BELOW The German pointer in possession of the toy has discovered that it's dull if no one else wants it. Meanwhile, the black-and-white pointer is waiting for a sign to leap to his feet and wrestle for the toy. Both dogs are in standoff, each waiting for just a tiny sign from the other (in the end, the German pointer caved in first).

 ABOVE Due deference. The retriever is unsure of the boxer so she's making herself low and insignificant.

TIMING IS IMPORTANT The retriever, above, appears to be in full retreat from the boxer. Actually, she's simply being savvy. The boxer is not a hugely confident dog, and tends to be readiest to play if the dogs around him have expressed their deference. By slightly exaggerating her body language, she's ensuring that he understands her position. Her timing is immaculate — had she pushily pressed for a game, she would probably have been given a sharp refusal. A minute or two after the picture was taken, though, she got what she wanted: the boxer consented to play with her.

LAST-CHANCE DEALS

Even if a disagreement goes as far as a full warning, there are still several steps to take before anyone gets hurt. The irrepressible fox terrier had been nagging the boxer to play — and the boxer wasn't interested. Eventually he moved beyond annoyance and issued a full-blown warning. For once, the fox terrier heeded it, and the boxer pursued him off the scene to make his point. This type of warning is issued relatively frequently — it goes a stage beyond exasperation but falls several steps short of full aggressive action. Dogs value their status, but most show a strong awareness of their natural place in the pecking order as a situation develops — relatively few will risk a full fight.

ABOVE Finally, the fox terrier has gone too far. He had been aggravating the boxer with his impervious pushiness for some minutes. First the boxer gave an unambiguous growl, then he gave a leap and a lunge. This is the face of a seriously annoyed dog: tight skin, tense muzzle and clear whites-around-the-eyes. All four paws are off the ground as he leaps forward.

LEFT The fox terrier made a speedy exit, but the boxer pursued him, with his head lowered, for a few yards, just to make sure he'd made his point.

But the fox terrier has no memory for bad moments. Two minutes later he's back annoying the boxer.

LEFT Pause in play. The retriever has decided to take down the action a notch or two in a game that is becoming uncomfortably intense. Lying down sends an unambiguous signal, but the fox terrier doesn't "read" her.

SETTLING DOWN

After any conflict short of a full fight, dogs usually settle down surprisingly fast. Elaborate warnings can be part of a lively game. Always look at the body language of both the dogs involved before deciding what's going on. Context is the key — what appears to be overly aggressive or mouthy behaviour on the part of one dog may be acceptable to another as part of the game. In this sequence, the warning is given mid-game; it is taken on board and assimilated without the game being ruined or play being brought to a halt. The most gifted canine communicators send unambiguous signals: "This is fun", "You're bothering me", "Stop it!" and "We can start again" might be a typical sequence. Less talented or less socialised dogs may communicate in a more mixed-up way. The fox terrier's impervious demeanour brings out the signing used by the dogs around him, but a confident dog will take the lead and won't be deflected.

LEFT A play-break didn't work, so the retriever tries some controlling paw work — pushing down on the fox terrier's neck.

LEFT Play resumed — the retriever's messages have been understood sufficiently for both dogs to rejoin the game.

FEARFUL AND DEFENSIVE

Unevenly matched play can create a tense situation. The well-socialised retriever will play with any dog who is willing to join her, but is able to administer a warning when one is really necessary — two-way roughhousing is fine, but when all the pushing is happening in one direction, she will take some time out and make sure that it is her decision when play starts again. With a less determined playmate, she keeps up encouraging chasing, but limits the body contact, making sure that the boxer feels in control of the situation. What you see is actually the retriever's ability to handle and control a situation with almost any other dog. The boxer isn't sure — that's a concerned glance; his tongue isn't lolling, and his forehead skin is slightly tight. There's an element of warning there, but it's not serious. With the fox terrier, the warning is all on the retriever's side. A huge range of factors affects who is acting as senior dog in any situation, and the same dog may change roles according to the setting, the circumstances or the company. Socially flexible dogs can work with the circumstances as they change; others are less malleable and try to hold on to their position, regardless of what is going on around them.

ABOVE The slightly uncertain terrier used disrespectful and domineering body language. The roughhousing is all coming from the terrier; the retriever, caught off guard, is forced into an awkward, hard-to-defend position.

ABOVE The retriever is still mid-chase, but the boxer has paused and is averting his gaze. He was enticed into play slightly against his inclination and is stopping every few seconds to cool down the game. In the gaps, he directs "hard" warning looks at the retriever.

APPEALS FOR HELP

A dog in a difficult spot will appeal to a higher authority. If he's a pet dog, his higher authority may turn out to be his owner. The dogs on these pages have exhausted their own resources and are looking to someone else to get them out of their undesirable situation. Learn to distinguish when you should intervene in dog relationships and when you should leave well alone. Often dogs will work things out themselves without any help from you, so give them the chance to do so. First, it's always best to reinforce good, brave behaviour in a pet. Breeders' lore is that you should choose the litter member who comes boldly to you and not the timid one who hangs back (although there is no hard research to support this). Still, you can reinforce confidence as a puppy grows up by ensuring that you pay no attention to mildly fearful

ABOVE This Jack Russell has planted her legs firmly and is dragging backwards against the leash. Her eyes are soft — this isn't a hard stare, it's a request for help.

reactions, but reward brave behaviour, so that it knows what gains approval and will be more likely to react accordingly. Second, if your dog turns to you in appeal, check out the situation carefully. If he's been playing with a group of dogs and has somehow sent the wrong signals, and the play is becoming intense and predatory, the likelihood is that you should break up the play instead of paying special attention only to your dog. If, however, your dog really can't cope with whichever outside factors are upsetting him — and remember, only the dog knows why he's so upset (you may think bright lights and a camera are no big deal, but your dog may be genuinely horrified by them) — then it's only fair to remove him from the situation that's causing his distress.

BELOW Rounded back, slightly puckered muzzle, lowered tail and steady look — all directed at her owner — send a clear message to "Get me out of here."

TAKING THINGS GENTLY

ABOVE These dogs meet nose to nose. The collie crossbreed gives a tentative greeting — look at the lowered tail and the slight paw lift.

Some gentle-natured dogs choose to avoid social situations until it is clearly safe to join in. These are the characters who voluntarily remain on the margins of a group, and who evidently prefer one-to-one interaction — but they may not always be the same dogs. Dogs decide what intimidates them, and their stress register may not accord with a human one, so look at the dog rather than at the situation before deciding how stressed he is. An exploding firework may be mildly disconcerting to one dog, but provoke a major freakout in another, and the level of stress is what matters, not what causes it. The collie crossbreed here is disconcerted by her surroundings and is using humble, unassertive phrasing. In response, the usually unassailable fox terrier has toned down his body language a little. He is still enthusiastic, but less ebullient in his greeting. This gentler approach holds the other dog through the preliminaries, but her nervous state means that she can't be enticed to play.

LEFT During a cautious mutual rear-sniff, the collie crossbreed's tail is still held low, while the fox terrier is as buoyant and upbeat as ever.

BELOW Just as the fox terrier decides it's playtime, the collie crossbreed decides that she wants out. She's holding herself low as she tries to sneak around him.

WARNING AND APOLOGY

The sequence of pictures here ends on an unexpected note. Puppy licking originates from primitive wild-dog behaviour that is still exhibited by wolves — in a wolf den, cubs lick their parents' faces to encourage them to regurgitate food for them. Puppies who have stepped over the line with an older dog "apologise" by anxiously licking the adult's face, reaching up from a low position. This emphasises their youth and diminishes any element of threat. Older dogs sometimes lick one another's faces in greeting or affection, too, but in these pictures the terrier is definitely mimicking the "apology" of a puppy, reaching up to lick the side of the boxer's face. The boxer does seem slightly appeased by the gesture — he's averted his gaze, withdrawing the hard stare he was levelling the terrier while they were in conflict. The fox terrier is particularly interesting to watch, partly because of the rapid-fire changes in his signing language and partly because of the extreme reactions he tends to provoke in other dogs.

BELOW As a warning, the boxer issues a forceful reminder to the fox terrier. His eyes and ears show that this is genuine irritation, not play. His face is forming the classic square-faced growl of a short-faced dog.

Perplexed for a few moments, the fox terrier stops what he's doing. There's a brief standoff between the two dogs.

LEFT The fox terrier apologises by going into a puppy-style routine, licking the boxer's face in a clear "I'm not a threat" gesture, and defusing the mood before going on to annoy him all over again. Note the boxer's averted gaze.

FINDING A WAY OUT

A dog who is uncomfortable with a situation — whether the cause is the proximity of unfamiliar dogs or people, or an environment in which strange things are happening — will usually leave the area if possible. If there isn't an exit he can take, he may try some other ways to relieve his stress. When a dog who is already showing slight signs of stress sits or lies down, don't assume that he's resting; chances are that he's sending a "no-threat" signal to those around him, as well as trying to deal with his own tension. Spinning in circles, sudden extreme grooming, scratching or sniffing are also common attempts to deal with stress. The collie crossbreed above backed herself into a tight corner before sitting down — making herself as comfortable as she could in an uncomfortable scenario. Other dogs may freeze and go still; this is different from the stillness a dog exhibits before some sudden action — it appears to be sent as an "I'm not here" signal.

● ABOVE The collie crossbreed, tired of repelling the terrier, and with no obvious exit, is using a sit as a calming gesture — probably for herself as well as the other dog. You can see the stress in her eyes and her facial tension. The terrier, by contrast, is pressing forward in a very forceful way.

◯ STRESS REACTIONS

If they can't get away from stress, some dogs react by resorting to exaggerated displacement behaviour. This little terrier, disliking her surroundings and told by her owner to stay put, reacted with a extreme sniffing routine. An onlooker might have assumed she had simply found a particularly fascinating smell; her uncomfortable body language, however, indicated that this was her solution to dealing with her stress levels.

◯ The boxer is directing a hard stare at his owner. He just wants to leave the scene.

TEST YOUR VOCABULARY

Try out your new reading skills with the eight photographs shown on these pages. All are casual snaps taken in a variety of situations, showing dogs you haven't met earlier in the book — so you can't use your insider knowledge of the dogs we've shown you along the way! Try to figure out what's going on in each picture (and whether, as a dog owner, you should be thinking of breaking things up in any of them). Don't go on "gut feeling"; collect your impressions by actually reading each dog's body language. Then turn to pages 122–123 to see how you did.

WHAT DID YOU SEE?

The collie is approaching the American bull terrier tactfully, slightly from the side. The other dog isn't comfortable with the approach — his ears are back and his face looks tense. In contrast, the collie is relaxed — her eyes are half closed, her ears are at half mast and there is no tension in her face. The terrier's owner isn't helping matters by holding the dog on a tight leash; if there is stress between two dogs, this will rarely help ease it. Despite the bull terrier's discomfort, this doesn't look like an imminent conflict, simply a slight wariness.

At first glance, these two dogs appear to be conscientiously ignoring each other, often a sign of discomfort in each other's company. However, look again — the dog on the left is a puppy, which may change the reading a little. It's more likely that he's imitating the stance of his elder — the pose is so close as to be almost a mirror image. Neither dog looks stressed, although both have ears forward and mouths closed, so they are probably waiting for the situation they're watching to develop a bit further before deciding whether action is necessary.

All these dogs are having a good time. The two exchanging the ball both have happy, open mouths, narrowed eyes and wagging tails. The sheepdog trying to intercept the ball is a little more uncertain — her mouth is wider and there's slightly more tension in her stance; however, although her tail is down, the topline of her back is relaxed. The terrier in the foreground can be read in one of two ways — either he's sending a relaxed "I'm not part of this" signal with his deliberate sniffing, or, just as likely, he has found something genuinely interesting to explore.

This is a slightly more complicated situation than in the previous picture. The black dog is trying a control hold with his paw on the dalmatian; his muzzle is crinkled with tension and his stance is as challenging as it is playful. The dalmatian is coming in under his chin, either for a feint to break his hold or for a play bite. Neither dog is altogether comfortable, but this still looks like a situation that will work itself out without human intervention. The spaniel is standing back (and keeping clear) while he assesses what the true position is.

In this classic hello, you might think that you can't tell much about the larger dog, because you can't see her face, but as the terrier moves in for an uncompromising introduction, the other dog shows awareness she's there (tail raised, allowing the other dog access, and slightly braced back legs). There's no apparent discomfort on either side — this might embarrass an owner, but the dogs are quite comfortable.

Despite the full-on contact, this is definitely play. The underdog has an open, relaxed mouth (lolling tongue) and a loose face. The braced paws look casual; this dog is rolling, not scrabbling to get up. And the play biting and snarling is happening side-on, not nose-to-nose. Both dogs are perfectly happy with their situation.

This isn't clearly play, as it was in the previous picture. The hound is averting his face slightly, but the shepherd dog is approaching as far as possible head-on, with a tense muzzle. His hackles (the central band of fur on shoulders and back) also appear to be raised, indicating a high state of arousal. The upright paws-on-shoulders position suggests a serious jockeying for status rather than the more relaxed side-barging seen in many games. All in all, an owner might do well to break this up now, by creating a diversion or calling his or her dog.

Not a trick picture — this is exactly the happy dog she appears to be. Open mouth, half-mast ears, happily raised tail and cheerful, squinting eyes all spell a dog who is ready for play action.

FURTHER INFORMATION

There are many intriguing books on reading dogs; what follows is a very short selection. Best of all are those titles that give you a real feeling of enlightenment as you see your dog's behaviour reflected — and you should find a number of them here.

BOOKS

The Body Language and Emotion of Dogs
Milani, M. M.
WILLIAM MORROW & CO., 1986

Bones Would Rain From the Sky: Deepening Our Relationships with Dogs
Clothier, S.
WARNER BOOKS, 2002

Canine Body Language: A Photographic Guide Interpreting the Native Language of the Domestic Dog
Aloff, B.
DOGWISE PUBLISHING, 2005

Dog Language: An Encyclopedia of Canine Behaviour
Abrantes, A., Rasmussen, A. and Whitehead, S.
DOGWISE PUBLISHING, 2001

The Dog Listener: Learn How to Communicate with Your Dog for Willing Cooperation
Fennell, J.
HARPERCOLLINS, 2004

Dogspeak: How to Learn It, Speak It and Use It to have a Happy, Healthy, Well-behaved Dog
Dibra, B., and Crenshaw, M. A.
SIMON & SCHUSTER, 1999

Dogwatching: Why Dogs Bark and Other Canine Mysteries Explained
Morris, D.
RANDOM HOUSE, 1995

How Dogs Think: Understanding the Canine Mind
Coren, S.
FREE PRESS, 2004

How to Speak Dog: Mastering the Art of Dog/Human Communication
Coren, S.
FREE PRESS, 2004

If Dogs Could Talk: Exploring the Canine Mind
Csanyi, V., tr. by Quandt, R. E.
SUTTON PUBLISHING, 2006

The Intelligence of Dogs: A Guide to the Thoughts, Emotions and Inner Lives of Our Canine Companions
Coren, S.
POCKET BOOKS, 2006

On Talking Terms with Dogs: Calming Signals
Rugaas, T.
DOGWISE PUBLISHING, 2005

The Rosetta Bone: The Key to Communication Between Humans and Canines
Smith, C.
HOWELL BOOK HOUSE, 2004

Tales from the Dog Listener: 28 Secrets to Being Your Dog's Best Friend
Fennell, J., and Roberts, M.
ULYSSES PRESS, 2006

You Are a Dog: Life Through the Eyes of Man's Best Friend
Bain, T.
HARMONY, 2004

WEBSITES

The following websites contain additional useful information:

aspca.org
rspca.org.au
rspca.org.uk
Websites for the societies for prevention of cruelty to animals in America, Britain and Australia. These include interesting articles as well as rescue and welfare information.

caninebehaviour.co.uk
The UK-based site of the Canine Behaviour Centre. Includes case studies and articles.

cleardogtraining.com
An Australian site with FAQs, articles and training tips.

dogbehaviour.com
The site of author and dog-behaviour specialist Gwen Bailey. Includes useful tips and information.

dogproblemsolutions.com
Advice and case studies on a range of behavioural problems.

dogpsychologycenter.com
Site of Cesar Millan, the star of the US Dog Whisperer TV show. Contains anecdotes, clips and case histories.

dogtech.com.au
Site of the Australian "Dog Whisperer". Includes articles and training tips.

dogwise.com
Comprehensive publishing site "for everything dog". Includes extremely wide range of dog-related books.

dvmnewsmagazine.com
News magazine of veterinary medicine, with up-to-date features and articles.

INDEX

ACKNOWLEDGEMENTS

With thanks to all the dogs and their owners, to Clare Barber, Calvey Taylor-Haw and to everyone else at the Ivy Press, particularly Kevin and Hazel.

Thanks, too, to Karen Overall for acting as such an informative and helpful consultant.

PICTURE CREDITS

iStockphoto/Galina Barskaya: **119 bottom**; Anna Bryukhanova: **118 bottom right**; Anne Clark: **118 top**; Brandon Clark: **120 top right**; dwphotos: **121 top**; Chris Johnson: **121 bottom**; C. Paquin: **119 top**; Ulrich Willmünder: **120 bottom.**